Manifesting

An Easy To Read Guide To Understanding And Applying
The Principles Of The Law Of Attraction

*(The Untold Truth About How To Make The Most Of The
Principle Of Attraction)*

Rüdiger Trummer

TABLE OF CONTENT

Prophetically Calling Forth Blessings To Be Bestowed On..1

Both Positives And Negatives Of The Situation 12

Acquire The Practice Of Feasting On The Word Of God. 16

Putting Everything Under One Roof....................27

Employ The Loa Tools. 36

Be A Contributor To The Team 41

Utilizing A Board For One's Vision.......................51

It Is Now Time For You To Walk In Victory.....56

You Can't Put Your Hopes For Success In Luck 81

A Rare And Valuable Assistance Being Granted 89

Advice On The Art Of Manifestation....................94

Keep A Good Mood And Attitude At All Times 99

Conclusion 104

Confidence In Oneself Is The Source Of The Power To Attract Others. 106

Having A Goal In Life While You're Here 115

Manifesting Joy 125

How To Bring More Money Into Your Life Is A Step-By-Step Guide 137

How Can One Make The Most Out Of Manifestation Strategies To Maximize Their Benefits? 143

Prophetically Calling Forth Blessings
To Be Bestowed On

ENCOURAGEMENT AND FINANCIAL SUCCESS

Then the King promoted Daniel, gave him many magnificent gifts, and named him ruler over the entire province of Babylon as well as chief prefect over all of Babylon's wise men... Daniel 2:48-49 (KJV)

Scripture teaches that there is no other source save the Lord from which one can advance in their career.Psalm 75:6-7 asks, "Who is it that can lift one off from the dunghill and seat him with princes?" The answer is God.,8th verse of 1 Samuel

It is now time to declare divine advancement and success in all that you accomplish in the year 2021 into your life. verse 23:5-6 states, "thou anointest my head with oil; my cup runneth over." His word also mentions this in verse 23. For surely, love and mercy are going to accompany me all the days of my life; and it is settled: I will abide in the house of the Lord forever...Psalm 23 verses 5-6

SAY THIS APPLICABLE PRAYER

a) Pray for divine promotion. b) Pray also for divine uplifting. c) Pray for the call of good news. d) Pray for the abrupt transformation. e) Pray for divine timing. a) Pray for divine promotion. b) Pray also for divine uplifting. c) Pray for the call of good news.

c) A BREAKTHROUGH ON THE FINANCIAL FRONT

"And My God Will Meet All Your Needs According to His Glorious Riches in Christ Jesus." Philippians 4:19 is cited.

God is the source of the available money resources. The flow of money is governed by forces that originate in the spiritual realm and work their way down into the material world. Peter followed Jesus' instructions and opened the mouth of the first fish he encountered in order to extract money from it. He was successful in doing so. Can you even fathom the possibility of fish having anything to do with making money? When you believe in God and put your trust in him to work, extraordinary things can happen. To bring it forth, the capacity to do so is inside your own words.

PRAYER DESTINATIONS

a) Pray for a financial breakthrough b) Pray for financial freedom c) Pray for hidden wealth to be transferred to you d) Pray for a sudden financial blessing from the Lord e) Pray for opened doors and abundant financial blessings a) Pray for a financial breakthrough b) Pray for financial freedom c) Pray for hidden wealth to be transferred to you d) Pray for a sudden financial

d) ANNOUNCE THAT YOU ARE IN GOOD HEALTH

This is my God, and I will praise him; this is the God of my father, and I will exalt him... The Lord is my strength and my song, and he has become my salvation. "The Lord is my strength and my song, and he has become my salvation."Exodus 15:2 (KJV)

God alone is the one who provides security and safety. As long as you put your faith in him to provide for you and your family, he will do so. Continue to speak well of the health of you and your loved ones. Always declare that your departure is blessed, and always declare that your arrival is blessed as well.

"The Lord will keep thee; the Lord will shade thee on thy right hand. You will not be struck by the sun during the day, nor by the moon during the night. The Lord will keep your spirit and keep you safe from any harm that may come your way. From this point forward and even into the foreseeable future, the Lord will protect both your outgoing and incoming journeys....verses 5-8 of Psalm 121

PRAYER POINTS a) Pray for good health. b) Pray that the LORD protects you and your family from any strange sickness or illness. c) Pray for inner peace and joy. d) Ask the LORD to protect you and your family always from evil arrows of sickness. e) Pray for divine strength. d) CLAIM DIVINE FAVOR "The king loved Esther more than all the other women, and she obtained grace and favor in his sight more2 Esther 1:7

Declare the divine favor in your life, and pray that God will guide your steps at all times. The words that come out of your mouth and the things that you express will always be respected by the lords. Therefore, you should be confessing positive things and believing that the Lord will bring it to pass in your life.

Therefore, I say to you, whatever it is that you ask for in prayer, believe that you have already received it, and it shall be given to you....Mark 11:24

Your petition will be granted by God if it is in accordance with his plans and purposes for your life and the course of your destiny. Your role is to keep declaring, to keep it in your tongue always until it happens, and to believe that it has already happened, for it is impossible to satisfy God without faith. Hebrews 11:6 is cited.

PRAYER POINTS a) Always pray for divine favor in your life. b) Pray for a special package from God to you. c) Pray for the surprise blessing of God in your life. d) Receive favor from both man and God. e) Always receive excellent and great news in your life. f) Pray that your life moves from glory to glory. g) Always pray for great joy and peace. PRAYER POINTS a) Always pray for divine favor in your

f) ADVERTISE YOURSELF AS YOUR DESTINY'S PARTNER AND HELPER

"Take delight in the Lord, and he will give you the desires of your heart." – Verse 4 of Psalm 37

I will utilize my experience as a way to testify to you using my tale. I have been daydreaming about the characteristics of my future partner for a number of years now while I look for her. I looked everywhere, including on Christian dating websites, because I wanted to find a pious woman as well as a beautiful one. I tried every possible venue. Everyone has an idealized vision of what they hope their future spouse would be like. I started talking to a few of them in the hopes that one of them might be mine someday. I prayed and hoped that it would happen. At that time, I never promised anyone friendship or marriage; rather, I encouraged them to do well in school.

Because you can see someone's outward look, but God sees the heart, there was a period where I reached a point where I was perplexed about it. The inner workings of a person's character can be concealed, but they can never be concealed from God.

I made the decision to give God the upper hand by abstaining from any sin that was associated with the situation and claiming Jesus as my partner both during the day and at night.

One day, the voice of God spoke to me and informed me that the answer to my search, which had taken me all over the world, over the internet, and to faraway places, was standing directly in front of me the whole time. I didn't realize this until the week that a buddy of mine might have introduced me to a lady that

I have met in my days of Evangelism, preached to her, and prayed for her without knowing that I was connecting with the woman who would eventually become my wife. I didn't grasp this until that week. Even though some of the qualities I look for in a partner are not present in her, I believe that God gave me his best rather than my best because we are now married and make a beautiful couple. He brought me a great deal of serenity and joy in the form of her, and I am thankful for the day that we married each other.

You can make the same claim to your divine companion this year if you allow God to have his way, and if you do so, you will receive the very best that God has to offer you. If you have faith in it, then you should start asserting it right away.

PRAYER DESTINATIONS

a) Pray for the right person to marry you. b) Pray for a divine connection. c) Pray for the peace of God in your life. d) Pray that your joy will never be taken away from you. e) Pray for divine provisions for those who are ready for marriage. f) Pray that God opens your eyes to see the right person. g) Pray for God's wisdom and understanding. a) Pray for the right person to marry you.

Both Positives And Negatives Of The Situation

In this chapter, you'll learn about some of the benefits of visualization as well as why it's vital to practice it. Visualization has a number of advantages, all of which will become clear to you after reading this chapter. For the time being, though, I will describe the benefits and drawbacks that I've discovered after putting my findings into practice, as I am confident that once you begin visualizing, you will come up with your own list of positives.

The Positives And Negatives

Relaxation can be achieved through the practice of visualization. The simple act of settling your thoughts and imagining something can significantly reduce the amount of strain that you are constantly subjected to throughout the course of a typical day. Therefore, even if you have never visualized before for any other purpose, I strongly encourage you to do so for this particular goal.

The practice of visualizing something that you would like to have or that you would like to experience might potentially bring a great deal of joy into your life. We might not be in a position to do or have what we wish right now, but we can still picture ourselves in that position.

This is the best thing that can be compared to really having it or carrying it out. Because our minds are unable to differentiate between seeing something and actually possessing or doing that item, they will respond in the same manner as they would if you were actually going through the experience that you are visualizing.

There are no boundaries when one is using visualization. You have the potential to become and achieve anything. You are able to get married to the person you have always dreamed of, drive the car of your dreams, live in the house of your dreams, and go to a variety of other places. The majority of us do not currently have access to this luxury; nevertheless, when we visualize, we have the power to visualize anything we desire, without any restrictions.

Visualization helps you improve your ability to focus because it forces you to empty your thoughts of distractions. You are freed from the constraints that your day previously imposed on you. The more you practice visualizing, and the more skilled you become at it, the more your overall focus will improve.

By taking the time to envision your goals, not only will you be able to obtain the motivation necessary to move forward with pursuing them, but you will also be able to become inspired to do so. If we can actually envision ourselves achieving our goals, we are more likely to believe that it is possible for us to do so, and this is something that we can accomplish through visualization.

It is difficult to identify any disadvantages associated with visualization. The most typical one is the amount of time that must be taken out of one's day in order to do the task. Nevertheless, taking this time could end up being quite useful.

Acquire The Practice Of Feasting On The Word Of God.

Because of their biological make-up, human beings have a constant need for nourishment to ensure their own survival. Without this, human people will not be able to develop properly or lead healthy lives. This is a truth that has been well-established. After this brief sojourn on earth, during which we are spiritual beings temporarily inhabiting physical bodies, we will make our way back to the spirit world, which is our true home and the place from where we originated. It is expected of us that we will feed and nourish our spiritual bodies in the same way that we feed and replenish our physical bodies through the consumption of physical food.

However, our spirit cannot consume the physical nutrients that we consume; rather, the word of God provides nourishment for the human spirit. It is necessary for us to cultivate the mentality of satiating ourselves on the word of God, because doing so will result in the growth of our spiritual senses, which is necessary for our manifestations as the redeemed people of God.

Read Jeremiah chapter 15 verse 16 Your words have been discovered, and I have digested them. Because I carry your name, LORD God of the Heavenly Armies, the words that you spoke brought me joy, and my heart was delighted. (ISV)

There are times when we find ourselves reading about the prophets of the Old Testament or even the apostles who were responsible for the beginning of the apostolic age of the church. There are occasions when we find ourselves pondering the possibility that these individuals have superhuman capabilities. However, beliefs like these are not accurate, and we need to educate ourselves on the strategies that led to their success. When you look at the Scriptures in great detail, you will find that they are talking about the relationship that the prophet had with the word of God.

The prophet was explaining to God how highly he had valued the words of God throughout his life. You may read the prophecy in the prophet's own words by clicking here: "Your words were found (talking about God), and I consumed them. Because I carry your name, LORD God of the Heavenly Armies, the words that you spoke brought me great joy, and my heart was filled with happiness. Beloved, are you able to utter a proclamation comparable to the one that the prophet has made? If at all possible, please let us give thanks to God for your life. If you can't, there's no need to be ashamed; just start from where you are, take one passage at a time, believe in God, store the word in your spirit, and utilize it in your prayers, meditation, and battles against the forces of evil.

Job 23: 12 I have not deviated from the instructions that he has given; I have cherished what he has spoken more than my own meals." (ISV)

Permit me to present another ancient text for your consideration. The book of Job is thought to be one of the earliest books in the Bible, according to the opinions of theologians. This holy man from the Old Testament had an extraordinary relationship with God. One day, during the times of his anguish, he publicly declared to God that ever since the day the angels of God delivered him the word of God, he has never neglected the holy word of God. He said this while he was in the midst of his suffering. When Job spoke these things, the trustworthy God answered to the petition of the man by delivering him from his trouble and increasing his wealth even farther than it had been before. You are able to perceive that the people of the old testament got the words from angels, and they honored the words as if they were the exact words of God, are you not?

We are all aware that nothing is impossible with God; hence, the Bible is packed with testimony about how people believed the word of God, clung to the word, and ruled human systems as well as the laws of nature by using the word of God. God is an integral component of the word. The will of God for every condition or situation in life can be found in the written word. The written word has the power to direct, guard, and direct you. Do not put off deciding to pay attention to what God says until you have direct experience with him in the shape of a physical being. The truth and authority of God's word have been firmly established in the heavenly realms. Because there is no possibility of it failing, you should make use of it. If you make the decision to let the word of God permeate your being, you will not be sorry for the rewards that come your way both in this life and the next.

Timothy chapter four verse six You will be a good servant of the Messiah Jesus if you continue to bring these things out to the brothers. You will be nourished by the words of the faith and the healthy teaching that you have followed diligently. (In the International Standard Version) This excellent passage of scripture is for the person who decides to enter into the ministry of the Lord. I have already stated that our spirits do not require physical food for survival although our bodies do. The word of God is the sustenance that sustains our spiritual bodies. As a direct consequence of this, holy workers of God ought to minister or preach the word of God with genuine zeal and enthusiasm. Preach the word of faith that will nurture the souls of others if you want to be a devoted servant of Jesus Christ the Messiah. The words of faith spoken by those who believe will transform them into instruments of service in the hands of the All-Powerful God.

1 Chronicles 1:8 This list of instructions is not to be excluded from any of your conversations in any way, shape, or form. Think about it constantly, both day and night, so that you may be sure to carefully carry out everything that is

mentioned in it; if you do this, you will be successful and prosperous. 9 You've been given instructions, haven't you? Maintain your fortitude and bravery. You are not to be afraid or disheartened, for the LORD, your God, goes before you and will be with you wherever you go. (In the International Standard Version) When we read the tale of Moses and Joshua in the Bible, we stop and question ourselves whether or not those works actually occurred. There are moments when we either have doubts about them or find it very difficult to embrace the fact that these miracles actually occurred as a result of the ministry of men. These were regular people who had the audacity to trust in a supernatural God and hold him to his word despite their beliefs. Recall that I have stated previously in this book that the revealed will of God can be found in the word of God. This indicates that God desires for you to have a complete understanding of what he has written in the Bible; doing so will provide you with the means to exercise dominion and achieve freedom in a world that is under the grip of Satan.

Shortly after Moses passed away, the God of Israel made an appearance to Joshua in order to explain the steps that Joshua needed to take in order to be successful in the new ministerial position that was going to be occupied by Joshua. The very first injunction that God gave to Joshua was that he should always have the word of God in his mouth, both during the day and the night. The second piece of instruction that God gave to Joshua was to make sure that all that was stated in the Bible was meticulously carried out. The next item that Joshua was to do according to God's instructions was to be strong, and the final instruction was that Joshua should have a lot of courage. After that, Joshua needs to have the epiphany that God is with him at all times and in all places, regardless of the circumstances. I feel that this message brings peace and solace to the hearts of all those who believe.

Do you know the reason why God commanded Joshua to reflect on the word of God both during the day and at night? Because I have a firm conviction that the Lord may be found in His words, it follows that the more time you spend reading the Bible, the more you will be exposed to the word of God. The instruction book for God's mission on earth is found in the Bible. It follows that if you want to be successful in this job of the ministry, you need to diligently follow the word of God from the very beginning of the Bible to the very conclusion of it, and then you can be certain that you will be successful in whatever it is that you are doing.

In addition, I am of the opinion that the written word of God serves as the guiding document for the administration of God's kingdom. As soon as you enter a new country, you will be subject to the law of that nation and expected to behave in accordance with its norms. It is the same way with the kingdom of God; the word of God will teach you how to access the resources that God provides and how to translate those into the natural world so that you can be fruitful with them. You must learn to spend time with the word of God, either by reading the Bible or listening to preachings that have been anointed, because the word of God is reliable.

Putting Everything Under One Roof

In order to live the life of your dreams, you must first be able to define what that life entails. Next, you must be willing to collaborate with the world in order to realize your goals, and last, you must remember that whatever the universe hands you, it is your responsibility to treat it with the utmost respect. You have to be willing to face the possibility that your opinion will shift as you come closer to achieving your primary objective. You have to come to terms with the possibility that the cosmos has something more beneficial in store for you. You must be conscientious about the upkeep of both your intellect and your life in order to achieve success. You must acquire the skill of asking, and then letting go, in order to let your oneness connection to perform the work that it must do without your interference. You have to be willing to acknowledge and accept miracles when they occur. You have to acknowledge that the law of attraction works just like magic, despite the fact that it requires some effort on your part.

You must make sure that you never lose track of your objectives. If you feel the need to do so, write them down; otherwise, find a way to remind yourself on a daily basis of the reasons you choose to go on this particular trip. You want a better life, you want to make changes that will lead you to the life you have always dreamed of, you want the roadblocks that have been stopping you from attaining your ambitions to disappear, and you want to witness miracles happen. You want all of these things to happen at the same time.

During the process of teaching myself the skills of manifestation, I had to ask myself on multiple occasions how these techniques were any different from any other technique that was available to me. I came to realize that it was far simpler to examine manifesting in terms of what it was not. It is not a religion, it does not require me to be a member of any organization, it does not require me to attend lengthy lectures or rallies, it does not cost me anything (other than my time), and it is not some kind of pyramid scheme leading to some kind of get-rich-quick plan. Your readiness to ask for what you need and your desire to form a relationship with a power that you believe to be larger than yourself, who created all things and is a part of all things, are the only specific needs. It is similar to Zen and the Christian faith, and it is global in nature. There are no additional conditions.

You will now be able to gain a grasp on how it operates because to the fact that the idea behind it, which is really rather simple, has finally been articulated. It's not all that different from making a wish on a shooting star or extinguishing the candles on your birthday cake, is it? In the course of our lives, we have always possessed the power to form wishes; the process of manifesting only compels us to adopt a more concentrated approach to the process.

The fact that the process may be completed with such relative ease is both a blessing and a curse. The exercises that were offered previously are tools that can assist you in learning to clear your mind. However, you do not need to perform these exercises each time you practice the art of manifesting because they are not required. When you realize that all you have to do is ask for whatever you want, whenever you want, and then go about your normal life, and all of a sudden your wish is realized! You are going to discover that the enchantment that lies within the ease of manifesting is in and of itself a miracle. There is no need to use any specialized equipment, spend hours with your hands clasped behind your head, or say any secret mantras. It will turn into a routine that you will begin to look forward to maintaining. This application does not require any further expenditures from your bank account or visits to look for specific objects because everything is taken from your heart and your memory. In no time at all, you will realize that you are manifesting without even thinking about it until whatever you desired appears in your life, at which point you will be reminded that you had, in fact, asked for it. Until that point, you will find that you are manifesting without even thinking about it.

The act of manifesting might bring you more money, improved health, or simply things that are more desirable than what you already have. But beyond all of the tangible items that you might possibly acquire in your lifetime, the act of manifesting ought to bring you mental tranquility, a reduction in stress, joy, and a sense of purpose within the larger scheme of things in the universe. It's possible that you aren't aware of how significant your role is in the world right now, but the universe is aware of your value. If you learn the skill of manifesting, the universe will demonstrate to you that you have a lot of worth. When you open your heart and mind to the opportunities that the universe has in store for you, you will experience a profound sense of oneness. This sense of oneness will bring you a serenity and peacefulness that great wealth cannot deliver. That doesn't mean you can't have both, though; what it does mean is that having a lot of money will feel pointless if you don't have somebody to share it with and you have to work hard to keep all you've got secure from other people. It is time for you to take a step back from your life and take a good, hard look at the obstacles that are standing in the way of you living the life of your dreams. Manifesting is about sharing your good fortune with others so that others can grow in the wisdom of the universe and learn of the gentleness of nature and the hope of a brighter future, the same things that you seek. It is time for you to select which directions you want to take in life and what sacrifices you are ready to make in order to realize the goals that you have set for yourself. It may be as easy as giving up some of your time, or it may be more complex and challenging, requiring that you turn your back on people and things that will not allow you to grow and practice manifesting in your life. Either way, it will require that you let go of whatever that is preventing you from practicing manifesting in your life. You are the only one who can decide what to do with these options. You may not need to make huge decisions all at once, but it should be evident to you by now that there are factors in your life that have hindered you from manifesting your dream life up to this point. It is time for you to make some changes so that you can live the life you have always imagined. Take advantage of this moment to make a move that will alter the course of your life for good. It is time for you to create a new life for yourself that is liberated from hopelessness, fears, worries, and concerns about the future.

Therefore, take a step forward into the light of the universe, and allow yourself to be filled with the love that is awaiting you. Put in your first request, and start living your life. I want for you that the miracles that occur in your life will be the beginning of something so amazing that you will feel compelled to share it with everyone person that you come into contact with. And may you be graced with the experience of magic each and every day that you travel through the oneness of the cosmos.

Employ The Loa Tools.

Affirmations of positivity and imaginative visualization are two applications of the law of attraction that will be of tremendous assistance to you all the way through this process. If you have faith in their capabilities, either of these tools will serve you well; in fact, they are based on the same fundamental idea.

First, let's have a better understanding of what these tools are and how they function, and then I'll show you how to use them.

Affirmations of the positive and visualizations of the creative

Any proposition that you place your faith in and consider to be the truth is referred to be an affirmation. A positive affirmation is a positive suggestion that you choose to believe is the ultimate truth and accept as the basis for your belief. When you put your faith in anything, it integrates itself into the way you think about things and is eventually acknowledged by your subconscious. When the subconscious mind accepts a suggestion, it incorporates that idea into your inner program. It then molds your thoughts in accordance with this new portion of your inner program, which in turn draws other, similar thoughts toward you.

Visualization, especially creative visualization, operates in a manner not dissimilar to this. It uses images to convince you of something, and when you put all of your faith in an imagination and give it all of your attention, you force your subconscious mind to acknowledge that what you imagined is actually the fact. Since you are aware that the subconscious is unable to differentiate between fact and imagination, it will take the image at face value and utilize it to guide the formation of your thoughts in accordance with its findings.

There is nothing that can stop you from receiving what you desire if you think positively and picture things in your mind's eye. The following outlines how you should go about practicing these two different strategies.

Instructions on How to Put Positive Affirmations Into Practice

To put positive affirmations into practice, focus on working through the following steps:

Consider your objective, and then create a reassuring affirmation that focuses on achieving it.

Make sure the affirmation has a positive tone and does not include any phrases that could be interpreted negatively.

Sayings like "I won't be sad" should be replaced with "I am happy."

The affirmation needs to have a present-tense focus, which means it should indicate that you are already accomplishing what you desire rather than implying that you will accomplish it in the future. stating things like "I will earn a million dollars" is not as effective as stating things like "I make a million dollars." When you do this, your subconscious will have the impression that it has already accomplished what you want, and it will work much harder to offer you positive experiences in the here and now.

Repeat the affirmation aloud while maintaining an air of self-assurance and total faith for a period of approximately ten minutes. Make sure that the vibration of every word rings in your ear so that you may concentrate entirely on what is being said to you and trust it.

You could even write it down as you speak it to help you concentrate more intently on what you are saying and increase the impact of what you are saying.

Do this every day, and make it a point to recite the intention you developed for your ultimate objective both in the morning and in the evening so that you can maintain your concentration on it.

Be A Contributor To The Team

Knowing how to collaborate with other people is probably the single most critical skill for a winner to possess. To be successful in life, you are going to absolutely need to make sure that you are collaborating with other individuals on various projects. There are simply too many moving parts and variables for one person to ever be able to achieve all of their life goals totally on their own. Find a group of people that are not only able to assist you, but are also willing to do so, as this is what you need to do.

Talk to the people in your family and your friends. When you are having issues or when you require assistance, the first persons you will want to contact are those two groups of people. They are the ones who will be there to help you no matter what, and that is why you want to make sure that you have numerous of these types of individuals in your corner at all times. They are the ones who will be there to help you no matter what. Have a conversation with your close circle of friends and figure out which of them may be properly categorized as members of your team and which of them are more likely to be temporary allies.

You need to make sure that you are the kind of friend that they can count on if they are going to support you and help you rise to the next level. This is the most crucial thing. You must be able to step up and assist them anytime they require it, and you must be ready and eager to do so. Being a friend to folks who don't necessarily have your back in the same manner as you do is going to turn out to be something that is really going to prove crucial in your life. You should make it a point to assist your coworkers, despite the fact that they might not always be willing to assist you in return. After all, you want to be a good employee.

Keep in mind, particularly when it comes to your work life, that there are those who are just concerned with looking out for number one. That you want to be available and willing to help people at work, even though you understand that you may not get any acknowledgment or compensation for your efforts, and that you want to be available. It also indicates that you don't want to be the one who blames someone else for something, even if it really is their responsibility. (Giving the facts in a way that is totally true and giving only the information that is necessary rather than embellishing or trying to talk yourself out of any trouble is the primary difference between being honest and throwing someone under the bus.)

Ensure that you are also being the better person by acting in this manner. This indicates that you wish to give credit where credit is due. It's a fantastic feeling when your boss recognizes your hard work and gives you a reward for it, but you shouldn't forget about all of the people who helped you get to that point in the first place. Your reward may be diminished in the here and now as a result of sharing the spotlight with others, but those individuals will remember what you did for them, and your boss is going to remember how glad you were to everyone else over your personal advantage because of how grateful you were to everyone else.

It goes without saying that in order to reach the stage where you are able to remember to thank your teammates, you first need to have teammates. That calls for you to ensure that you can collaborate effectively with the other people around you. It is essential to ensure that everyone has the opportunity to express their thoughts and that everyone has an equal say in the decisions that are made during the cooperation. Naturally, the degree to which you are able to collaborate well with others is likely to be influenced by a wide variety of skills. Listening, public speaking, taking the initiative, and organizing will all fall under this category. The farther you are able to develop these skills, the more effectively you will be able to collaborate with other people.

Because not everyone is easy to collaborate with, you will need to possess skills in problem solving as well as patience in order to engage effectively with various types of individuals. When you are able to operate as part of a team, you are more prepared and more capable of achieving the goals that you have set for yourself, your company, or your family. This is true whether the goals are personal or professional. This is due to the fact that the greater the number of individuals working together on a project, the more successful it will be overall.

A winner is able to collaborate with a wide variety of individuals, and they are able to comprehend how to make the most of the greatest skills that each individual brings to the table in order to make the most of what they need to achieve. You will get the opportunity to interact with new people, get to know them better, and meet new people all while demonstrating some of your management talents to your supervisor. In the end, you receive a job that is finished better than you could have done on your own, and your boss sees you as an even bigger asset for the effort that you've put in and how you achieved it. This is a win-win situation for everyone involved.

Join up the dots

Connecting with the part of yourself that is not concerned about things like paying the bills or being devoured by a saber-toothed tiger is the most important step in mastering this aspect of the D.I.C.E. acronym. To put it another way, your more evolved self.

If you are a spiritual person, you can choose to think of this as establishing a connection to the greater cosmos. It's possible that if you are a religious person, you'll see it as a way to connect with God. It doesn't really matter as long as you are able to find what I refer to as the "sweet spot," which is when your mind is so calm, elevated, and absolutely persuaded that you are IN the vision you are visualizing that you are completely unaware of the room you are sitting in since your body is completely relaxed.

You may just think of it as the point in time when you feel most at ease when you are meditating deeply. Keep in mind that quantum research has shown us that there is in fact a pervasive electromagnetic field that is made up of energy and that it surrounds everything. And of course, on a neurological and psychological level, it is a fact that our subconscious thoughts are just out of our reach; nevertheless, when we are in this altered state of physical and mental relaxation, we are able to speak with this part of ourselves and impress ideas upon it. Do you recall the Folsom Dam? The subconscious mind is the doorway to higher states of consciousness as well as the quantum field, which is the location of all possible outcomes at the present moment.

Therefore, regardless of how you decide to engage and approach the connecting component, it is entirely OK to simply claim that you are "connecting" when you are in an environment that is characterized by inner calm and tranquility. This is significant because when you reach "that sweet spot" in which your imagination has become more real in your internal world than any existing state in your outer world, you are actually altering the physical structure of your brain. This is the point at which your imagination has become more real in your internal world than any existing condition in your outer world. Now we get to the part where the magic really starts to happen.

Utilizing A Board For One's Vision

This is somewhat similar to the boards that are used during conferences to highlight particular points that someone is trying to clarify to the audience. The purpose of this is to put your desire front and center on the board so that you can see all of the positive changes that will be brought about in your life as a result of pursuing it. It's almost like getting a clearer picture of what you want your life to look like. You are going to make use of this on a daily basis in order to make an effort to achieve what you believe is necessary in your life. After you have sketched out your plan and given it the attention to detail it requires, sit down in front of the board and take in all of the data. Next, close your eyes and act as though you already are the person you envision yourself to be. It is not enough to have a goal in mind; you also need to have the correct frame of mind, and the only way to achieve this is to believe in your dream and work toward making it a reality.

For instance, a person who is seeking a promotion at work but continues to conduct themselves in the same manner that they have in the past will not be successful in obtaining that promotion. It is clear that the plan was unsuccessful because other individuals received promotions while he did not. However, if he creates a vision board on which he lists all of the characteristics of a successful person who is suitable for management and then imagines himself in that position, there is a good chance that he will attract the attention of the higher-ups at the company, who may then decide to promote him. Consider the situation in this light. What use does it serve for him to be envious of other employees who obtain promotions if they are given? That will only serve to stoke the flames of hatred. He is unable to get along with other employees, and as he constructs a barrier of separation between himself and those who have been promoted, he demonstrates that he is not composed of the kind of material that would be regarded for a managerial job. However, with the use of a vision board, he would acquire the skill of congratulating his coworkers on promotions whenever they occurred. He will acquire the knowledge necessary to comprehend what it is that the managers desire in an employee and will begin to model his behavior after that ideal candidate. The principle known as the Law of Attraction ensures that this will be successful. Consider your options and decide which ending you'd prefer.

People who make comments of this sort tend fail to maintain the promises they make, which is why it is no longer sufficient to say "I am going to..." in this day and age. BE that person and prove by the positive changes that you make that you ARE that person, and any desire that you have ever had can come true. BE that person and show by the positive changes that you make that you ARE that person. You need to picture yourself taking pleasure in all of the things that are important to you, first in your mind's eye and then by putting your faith in those images. When you do that, it will affect the way you think, and those around you will notice the difference. This is not a game of make-believe. Simply said, it is a matter of realizing the potential that has always been present in the first place.

It Is Now Time For You To Walk In Victory

This is the moment for you to celebrate your win. It's possible that you've spent your entire life feeling dejected, if you've struggled to make ends meet and have gone from one obstacle to the next. Living a life that is consistently difficult may cause one to question whether or not the benefits of living are worth the effort.

The anguish that you are experiencing right now will ultimately serve to fortify you tomorrow. Always keep in mind that whatever challenges you face in life, everything ultimately works out for the best in the long run. This is true no matter where you are in life. Try not to become defeated by difficult circumstances. Learn to perceive adversity as a friendly sparring partner whose goal is to make you stronger and better and teach yourself to see it that way. Don't let the struggles of life make you feel helpless and overloaded. Walk in victory, for this moment has been ordained for you to achieve victory.

Master the art of celebrating your victories and thinking like a winner.

When it appears like all of the odds are stacked against them, a champion does not give up because they are confident that they will finally prevail. They never allow themselves to lose hope and refuse to give up until they have achieved the success they seek in their attempt.

Even when there appears to be no way out, think of yourself as a champion. When you decide to conduct your life based on your decisions rather than the outcomes of random events, you'll find that more and more opportunities arise to help you succeed. Don't just roll over and accept whatever it is that life throws at you; instead, decide what it is that you want to anticipate from life, and you will have nothing less. You have the ability to make a decision now that will affect the rest of your life and determine whether or not you will live a life of triumph or defeat.

Modify the way you now view yourself.

The way in which you think of yourself is of utmost significance. Your thoughts are a direct representation of who you are. If you think of yourself as a winner at all times, you will behave and perform like a winner in any situation. However, if you think of yourself as a victim, you will continue to be a victim no matter what the circumstances are.

Make a shift in your point of view. Imagine that you have already won the battle. Refuse to see yourself as a victim in any circumstance you may find yourself in. Only you have the power to decide whether or not you will allow yourself to be a victim of your environment. Your determination to succeed at all you do will serve as a barrier between you and disappointment. It will determine the manner in which people interact with you moving forward. You won't be seen as someone who can be taken for granted since people will see the value and significance that you bring to the table. Modify the way you now view yourself.

Gain wisdom from your past errors.

We are all capable of making errors. It is acceptable to act foolishly so long as one draws wisdom from their blunders. It's not so much the error itself that matters as how you respond to it, what you take away from it, and how you incorporate what you've learned into your daily life going forward. Always keep in mind that the most important lessons in life are frequently those that are discovered at the most inopportune moments and via the most embarrassing failures.

It is evident that you are not doing anything if you are not making any errors. Do not let the worry that you could make a mistake prohibit you from doing something with your life that will have a significant influence. Someone who did not go forward because they were afraid of making a mistake and did not pursue their objective is far further behind than someone who did pursue their goal despite making a large number of blunders.

In order to emerge victorious, you must first gain wisdom from your failures. It is to your advantage to gain knowledge from past errors, but it is detrimental and destructive to cling to those errors.

Put the past in the past and get on with the rest of your life.

Don't let something that happened in the past spoil the rest of your life. Put the past in the past and get on with the rest of your life. When you let go of the things that have happened in the past, you open the door for yourself to enjoy the gifts that are in your life at this very time.

Always keep in mind that you can't change what happened in the past. Whatever transpired in the past is beyond your ability to influence, and there is nothing you can do to change it at this point. Figure out how to make the most of the here and now. No matter how difficult it may appear to move on with your life, you should always keep in mind that until you fully let go of the past, you will never be truly free to live your life to the fullest. This is true even if moving on with your life seems impossible. You can't change what happened in the past, so stop dwelling on it.

You must put your trust in God.

If you place your trust in God, you will never be defeated in the battles you face. Put your complete reliance and hope in God, and don't rely on your own knowledge or wisdom. Since God is the one who started and completed our religion, he understands us better than we understand ourselves. He is aware of the difficulties we face and is aware of how to rescue us from those difficulties.

Having faith in God affects every aspect of one's life. When you place your complete trust in God, he will shower all of his good things on you. Without the presence of God, there is no such thing as a real victory. Acquire the habit of placing your trust in God, and

Encouraged Behavior

You now know that your brain contains a RAS that is responsible for working to direct your focus. You can see more possibilities, luck, and coincidences if you aim your focus in a certain direction. But if you don't do anything to go toward your goals, you won't get anywhere. An amazing activity is going to be taught to us now, so get ready for that! Put your dream into action by tapping into your intuitive abilities.

Many people hold the belief that only a select few individuals are in possession of the magical power of intuition. That is not the case. One of the things that the subconscious mind is responsible for is intuition. So there you go with that. You are gifted with intuition.

According to the definition found in the online version of the Oxford dictionary, intuition is "the ability to understand something instinctively, without the need for conscious reasoning." Therefore, the capacity to know or grasp something without resorting to analytical thought is what we mean when we talk about intuition.

If you wish to grow your company, you can quickly know how to do so, as well as what steps to do soon after that. The capacity for intuitive action is what we refer to as inspired action. When you follow your instincts and do what seems right, you are actually listening to the guidance of your subconscious mind.

This is the key distinction between inspired action and the type of activity that is frequently covered in other works on the subject of motivation. When you follow a muse and put your ideas into motion, it's as if you've entered a superhighway where you can speedily and effortlessly realize all of your ambitions. If you are having difficulty with your action, it is clear that you are heading in the incorrect direction. You must have faith in your innate senses.

When you are in a state of relaxation, your intuition will be able to connect with you. If you've ever watched an episode of The Secret, you're probably aware that Jack Canfield had the inspiration for how to make his first $100,000 while he was in the shower.

When I was confronted with a challenge and found myself at a loss for solutions, all I had to do was clear my thoughts before inspiration struck. They were wonderful suggestions to consider. It simply remains for me to carry it out.

Therefore, it is highly recommended that you learn how to meditate. However, many people claim that they just do not have the time to sit quietly and meditate. I have a technique that can assist you gain answers from the subconscious mind if you are one of those people.

Dream With a Predictive Meaning

Your intuition can speak to you through your physical sensations, your internal dialogue, your feelings, and your dreams. There are a lot of people who think it's ridiculous or mysterious to believe in their dreams. Despite this, we are well familiar with the concept of precognitive dreams and dreams that end up coming true.

Your conscious mind stays dormant when you are sleeping, allowing your subconscious mind to have unhindered access to your awareness while you are asleep. Dreaming is one way in which your subconscious mind can interact with your conscious consciousness.

We are only going to learn how to extract information from our dreams; therefore, we are not going to learn about more in-depth topics such as having lucid dreams or figuring out what our dreams mean.

In a nutshell, your subconscious mind interacts with you directly and does not require any further interpretation on your part. The next thing for you to do is either to carry out what you have been dreaming of or to follow up on what you have been planning. Your dream may give you with an answer, either directly or indirectly.

Let us assume that you are interested in expanding your company. The example that best illustrates the direct answer is the scenario in which you dream that you are going to see an old buddy. Find him as soon as possible, because you never know whether or not he will be able to assist you in this situation. If you lose contact with someone, make an effort to look for them. You may search it up on Facebook, Twitter, or Instagram, among other social media platforms. In today's world, social media has shown to be incredibly helpful.

If you are dreaming that you are playing the piano, this is an example of an indirect answer. It's possible that if your company has nothing to do with music, you won't find the response particularly helpful; nevertheless, who knows. Why not look into the piano, take some piano lessons, or enter a piano competition? that knows, from there you could be able to get to meet people that could end up being able to assist you in the development of your firm. There is no way for us to know what God has planned for us; all we can do is surrender.

You can employ The Magic 30 Minutes or the thirty minutes right before you go to sleep in order to acquire answers from your subconscious mind through the medium of dreaming. A dream could be prompted at such moment by sensualizing or reinforcing anything.

I know you must be thinking, "Wait, what if I'm not dreaming?" and I'm going to answer that question for you. You have got to be kidding me! Each and every night! It's likely that you have some kind of sleeping condition if you don't dream at all.

During the time that we are asleep, our bodies move through a total of five stages: four stages of non-REM sleep and one period of REM sleep. The first stage of sleep, known as light sleep, is when a person begins to relax and shuts their eyes. In the second stage, eye movement is permanently halted, and the speed of brain waves gradually slows. Deep sleep, also known as delta sleep, refers to stages 3 and 4 of the normal sleep cycle. Following stage 4, the Rapid Eye Movement, or REM, stage begins. This is the phase in which dreaming takes place.

These five stages progress in a circular manner, moving from stage 1 all the way to REM and then back to stage 1. Following the 70-90 minutes that are devoted to stages 1, 2, 3, and 4, REM sleep will take place for around 10 minutes. On average, it takes between 90 and 110 minutes to complete one cycle. The cycle repeats itself a total of six times during the course of one night. This indicates that we can have anywhere from four to seven different dreams in a single night.

When a person sleeps normally, they will have at least one dream. If you aren't having dreams, you most likely have some kind of sleeping condition. If a person goes several days without dreaming, it is likely that they will develop psychological and emotional issues. If you claim that you do not dream, this indicates that you have forgotten that you are actually dreaming. We are able to recall about 10% of the information contained in our dreams. Within the first five minutes of waking up from sleep, the majority of our dreams are immediately forgotten. After ten minutes, we are unable to recall ninety percent of our dreams.

So it is that you dream! The issue is that you forget about it. Therefore, before going to bed, get a pen and paper ready and place them next to you on the bedside table. If you wake up and can still recall aspects of your dreams, you should start writing down those details as soon as you can.

You might also try engaging in some form of self-hypnosis to help you remember your dreams. It shouldn't be hard to bring up memories of your dream. Once you have reached the hypnotic state, you should ask your unconscious mind for assistance in recalling a dream you had that may contain the solution to the issue you are having. As soon as you feel yourself entering a trance, speak to your subconscious mind and tell it, "I want to see my dream that contains information to resolve (your problem)." Please let me experience that dream once more so that I can remember it and comprehend it.

Due to the fact that your subconscious mind is not familiar with logic, the dream will not be 100 percent accurate or will not always provide the correct response. Therefore, the response you get could be completely ludicrous at times. Do not quickly dismiss the information as "useless" if the response you get is not the one you were hoping for. Because it is possible to upset your subconscious mind, causing it to stop wanting to assist you in the future.

Tell your subconscious mind that "this answer cannot help me" whenever you get a response that is either ridiculous or not very helpful. Will you provide me with another response?

After you have succeeded in calming your mind, the next thing you need to do is go on to the second phase, which involves learning to differentiate between positive and negative thoughts. This will allow you to eliminate the negative thoughts from your mind and concentrate on being more optimistic.
You won't be able to achieve your objectives so long as you let negativity get in the way.
You have not been effective in materializing your ambitions and dreams because there is something

wrong going on in your head, which is the reason for this failure. As soon as you are able to calm your mind a little bit, you need to figure out the blockages that are preventing the normal and good energy flow from your mind to the universe. These blocks are also causing an obstruction in the manifestation of your goals. Once you have identified these blocks, you will be able to move forward with the process of manifesting your goals. These negative blocks are basically all of the limiting beliefs that you have created and strengthened in your mind over the years. These beliefs lead you to believe that you are unable to do something that you wish, and as a result, you allow yourself to be held back by them.

A limiting belief is an ideology or a notion that claims you cannot move beyond a particular limit and that you cannot advance and groom yourself. Limiting beliefs can also be referred to as self-limiting beliefs. For instance, having the emotion or thinking, "I can never become an established entrepreneur," or "I am a complete loser," are both examples of limiting beliefs. These thoughts and feelings make you believe that you do not have the essential skills and talents to do something and bring your goals into reality. These beliefs are the ones wrecking havoc in your head and preventing a positive flow of energy from reaching its full potential. These specific ideas are the ones that need to be eliminated from your way of thinking in order to rid it of all of its negative connotations.

Self-Empowering Beliefs are Beneficial to Your Personal Growth.

There is a belief system that can provide you with wings and help you soar to great heights, in contrast to the beliefs that restrict your potential and stunt your development. These beliefs are referred to as self-empowering beliefs, and their purpose is to assist you in gaining an understanding that you, and only you, have the ability to advance in life. Your thoughts are the only thing that can either make or break you, and if you direct them in the right direction, you can certainly empower yourself. Your thoughts have the power to either make or break you. Beliefs that empower you to take care of yourself give you hope and open your eyes to new opportunities. They help you understand that you are on the same level as anyone else in this world, and that you have the potential to improve yourself and advance in life.

For instance, self-empowering beliefs include concepts such as "I have what it takes to become a world-class chef" or "I am capable of becoming a great motivational speaker." Other examples of self-empowering beliefs are "I am capable of becoming a great motivational speaker." These ideas give you the impression that you are able to act on the desires of your heart, pursue your aspirations, and one day truly give them the form that they take in reality.

Roger Bannister is a well-known athlete who is credited with being the first person to finish a mile race in less than four minutes. He did this by breaking the previous record. Before Bannister set this record, researchers had published studies claiming that no one could run a distance of one mile in less than four minutes. Bannister broke this record in 1954. Roger Bannister made the decision to make a difference and began putting in a lot of effort to train himself to break the record. In 1954, he was the first person to finish the race in under four minutes, which was an incredible accomplishment. When asked about the basis for his success, Bannister said unequivocally that it was his self-empowering beliefs that provided him with the bravery and strength to believe in himself and achieve this victory. He also attributed his achievement to the fact that he was able to believe in himself. After witnessing Roger's incredible success, other athletes started to have faith in themselves and began cultivating beliefs that are empowering to the individual. The following year, many more competitors were successful in beating Bannister's record, demonstrating to the world that having confidence in one's abilities is the most important factor in achieving one's goals.

This indicates that you can free your mind of all the mental barriers of negativity that are holding you back and let go of all the pent-up stress in order to become more upbeat and positive than you were before. You can do this by exchanging your self-limiting beliefs for beliefs that empower you.

Learning to Tell the Difference Between Positive and Negative Thoughts

It's not that difficult to recognize both good and negative thoughts and to differentiate between the two types of thinking. Spending some quality time by yourself and being persistent in recognizing the obstacles that are holding you back are the only things you need to accomplish. The following is what you are need to do:

• Grab a notebook and some writing implements, and head to a secluded area where no one can annoy you.

• Take a moment to get into a comfortable position and return to the method of mindful breathing that you regularly employ. After you have done it for approximately ten minutes and have calmed your frayed nerves, you need to allow your thoughts flow normally so that you may move on.

• Make sure that your journal has two columns. The first one ought to be labeled "Negative Thoughts," while the other ought to be called "Positive Thoughts." If you come across a thought that includes a negative term such as "no," "never," "not," or "incapable of," or if you come across a thinking that seems like a self-limiting belief, jot it down and file it under the "negative thoughts" category. If you have a self-enhancing thought pop into your head, jot it down and file it away in the 'positive thoughts' section of your journal.

• When you have finished writing down all of your ideas, you should then begin verbally reciting the ideas that are included in both columns to yourself. Take note of how the negative ones make you feel and write down in as much detail as possible how you are feeling. After that, repeat the same with the positive ideas. Going through your negative ideas will give you the sensation that you are being held back, and you will notice that your thoughts are preventing you from making progress. When you read your positive ideas, on the other hand, you will have a good feeling about yourself, and you will genuinely have the feeling that you can get better. You will have a better understanding of the incredible power of positive thinking by engaging in this straightforward activity.

As soon as you begin to experience positive and cheerful emotions on the inside, it is time to advance to the next practice in order to further enhance your positivity.

Getting Rid of Unhelpful Beliefs and Increasing Positive Thoughts and Attitudes

Since you are now capable of distinguishing your good and negative ideas from one another, it is time that you began the process of entirely releasing and removing the negative beliefs from your mind. By doing this, you will be able to make more room for the constructive thoughts and give them more weight in your life. The following is what you are need to do:

• Take the negative belief inventory that you prepared earlier, or you could write down your thoughts as they come and then start converting them into positive thoughts. Change the phrase "I am not good enough to be a chef" to "I am good enough to be a chef" if you have previously stated something along the lines of "I am not good enough to be a chef."

• Keep doing this till you have changed all your unconstructive thoughts to healthy ones.

• The next step is to verbalize and rehearse your newly formed ideas as often as possible while maintaining a positive attitude. You might also jot down any thoughts that are related to a certain subject or to any of your objectives in a journal. For instance, if you have the dream of one day running your own company but you have doubts about your ability to achieve this goal, you should write down all of the unhelpful thoughts associated with this goal, and then replace them with more empowering beliefs. Continue to read and write down your thoughts until you begin to feel like they are being ingrained in your head. Affirmations are healthy ideas that are offered to a person's subconscious, which is why this exercise is also known as practising positive affirmations.

It is essential that you use this tactic at least once per day for a period of twenty minutes. After around two weeks, you will notice that your mind is shifting toward a more optimistic outlook. When you begin to think less in a negative direction, you will begin to feel confident about yourself and your talents, and you will also feel less stressed than you did in the past. When you begin to think less in a negative manner, you will feel strong.

You Can't Put Your Hopes For Success In Luck

When it comes to the acquisition of riches, there is an allure to taking quick ways. Consider, for instance, the purchase of a lottery ticket. You have the chance of winning millions, yet it will only cost you a small amount of money to participate. On the other hand, it is a straightforward way to lose money. It is simple to fantasize that you will be a winner when you have no money or very little money, and while this is a possibility, there is a good reason why this should be considered a fantasy.

To begin, the probability of success is not in your favor at all. The amount of digits that need to be chosen and the possible values for those digits both play a role in the degree to which the chances are stacked against you. In addition to the possibility that you will need to engage in the lottery more than once, which will inevitably result in increased financial outlay, you are not required to purchase additional lottery tickets, and it is not clear why you would choose to take part in the lottery in the first place.

Tickets for the lottery are another potential silver bullet that could speed up the process of reaching your financial goals. There is an entire industry that preys on those who are desperate for money right now, and it includes anything from gambling to get rich quick schemes. They benefit more from your relationship with them than you do from theirs. You might then question, well, what options do I have?

You have the best and safest chance of success if you are prepared to undertake the actual work. You have to choose one strategy that you believe will be successful, and then you have to concentrate on that strategy until it is either successful or until experience demonstrates that it will not be successful, in which case you have to abandon it. Stop squandering your hard-earned money on unattainable goals and start putting in the effort if you want to be successful.

The key to success is putting in a lot of effort.

Anyone who wants to be successful must be willing to work hard for it since that is the price that must be paid, the majority of the time. One definition of "working hard" is "the diligence to labor and to complete tasks directed toward achieving a particular goal." This definition captures the essence of "working hard." We live in a time when the value of clever work may be more highly regarded than the value of hard labour. Work that is smart implies examining the duties that are expected of you and focusing your efforts on the activities that will advance you forward the most.

A lot of people put in a lot of effort every day, but they focus their efforts on chores that are routine and boring rather than giving priority to the activities that will have the most significant impact. You are going to continue to put in a lot of effort, but you are going to be more careful about where you put that effort. Therefore, any and all references to hard work should be understood to mean diligent, focused, and thoughtful work. When putting in a lot of effort, there are a few essential things you need to make sure you do.

It is essential that you dream large and that you make goals for yourself. You put a lot of effort into achieving your goals. It is a waste of time to force oneself to labor each day without having any kind of destination in mind. If you do not have criteria to use in evaluating your jobs, it is actually hard to differentiate between significant and trivial labor. In reality, it is impossible. When you have objectives, you need to divide them up into daily and weekly plans of action to achieve them. The method of breaking down goals requires conducting an analysis to determine which tasks will move you closer to achieving your goals more quickly and then allocating those duties to yourself on a regular basis. Putting in hard work means making sure that you adhere to this plan regardless of the circumstances. It is essential that you come to a choice and that you stick to it no matter what.

It is not the act of deciding that compels you to work toward a goal when you have one; rather, it is the commitment to the outcome of your efforts that does so. You need to demonstrate dedication to the plan that you have created as well as the daily activities that you have determined to be significant. If you have made the decision to launch your own company and have come to the conclusion that it is essential for you to educate yourself every day on topics such as business management and financial management, it is your dedication to reading on a daily basis that will truly lead to an increase in your level of expertise. After all, a lot of individuals make resolutions for the coming year on New Year's Day, but only a small percentage of them actually follow through with them. Your endurance will develop as a result of your commitment since you will not allow yourself to be defeated when things go wrong. In the end, those who are willing to commit are the ones who are successful.

You need to be open to gaining experience if you want to have any chance of becoming successful. Some people fall prey to a cognitive snare when they attempt to learn. They want everything to be just right before they begin. They never actually go out into the world to gather experience because they spend their days preparing, reading, and generally trying to avert any problems they believe they will encounter in the future. It is not a terrible thing to desire to be prepared; nevertheless, the future is unpredictable, and at some point you will have to put in the effort to do the actual tasks. Remind yourself that while setbacks are unavoidable, they do not have to be game-ending. In order to improve your skills, you must be willing to experience some setbacks along the way. You can amass as much academic expertise as your heart desires, but it will never be able to compare to the value of real-world experience.

You must be willing to network with other people. Get out there and talk to people that are employed in the same industry as you are. You can even go see folks who disagree with your opinions if you have the courage to do so. others who agree with you will tell you what they know and what they have tried in the past that was successful, but others who disagree with your ideas will encourage you to consider new ways to grow your brand so that they, too, may profit from it. However, keep in mind that you can't cater to everyone's preferences.

You will be able to form positive relationships with a variety of people if you participate in networking activities.

You can learn all you want to learn and become an expert in your profession, but you should always keep in mind that the money you want is with other people. If you choose to isolate yourself from the world instead of engaging it and forming meaningful connections with other people, your chances of being successful will be lower.

A Rare And Valuable Assistance Being Granted

In the life of Nehemiah, who was a slave in a foreign place and worked as a cupbearer to a certain monarch there, fasting resulted in extraordinary blessings being bestowed upon him. You, too, may find that fasting results in uncommon favors being bestowed upon you. He was moved by mercy in his heart to fast and seek the face of God for the revival of his nation, and God granted him an uncommon favor before the king and divine protection as they were rebuilding the wall of Jerusalem. When the news reached him that the wall of Jerusalem had been broken, as well as the affliction of his brethren, he was moved by mercy in his heart to fast and seek the face of God.

You will receive favors from sources that you did not anticipate receiving them; you will receive divine provisions and the protection of God, as it is said in the Bible in Proverbs 10:22, "the blessing of the LORD makes a person rich, and he adds no sorrow with it."

Nehemiah started out with nothing, but after he completed that fast, God blessed him by causing the king of that land to show him favor, set him free, and provide him with a great deal of provisions. When I read this verse, the story always stirs emotion inside me because I am aware of how Nehemiah lived his life and of the effects that prolonged fasting can have on a person. The man's life was transformed, the same king that he served started serving me, making sure that he puts a smile on the face of Nehemiah, this is what only God can do and this proves his word right in Proverbs 16:7 "When a man's ways please the LORD, He makes even his enemies be at peace with him"

God's word never fails, and when one applies the simple principle that He has given us, then you will see everything working right and perfect. He took the action that many others might have taken, but they were at a loss on how to proceed. When the news came to Nehemiah, however, he turned the bad news into good news by engaging in prayer and fasting. This enabled him to turn the situation around and produce a positive outcome. Don't feel like all hope is lost when situations comes, trust in him, and encourage yourself always in him like David did when he faced terrible situations. We need to learn more from this story and trust in God more having in mind that nothing can take him by surprise, so when he allows things to happen, HE does that sometimes to redirect us back to him, or show us that he is able to do all things. This is something that we need to keep in mind when we trust in him more. I've seen his mercy and kindness many times in my life, both in my marriage and in my finances, and I encourage you to fast frequently and to dedicate all to him; he will never fail you down. I have also improved my prayer and fasting life because I believe that to be one of the primary factors in one's level of achievement.

This type of fast can be done for three days, beginning at six in the morning and ending at six in the evening, and you are breaking the fast with fruits for each day. Alternatively, you can fast for three days straight with only water and no food at all. In this scenario, you are not only seeking the face of God for the solution to your own problem, but also for the solutions to the problems of others, such as those of your family, relatives, friends, business partner, or church of God. You are asking God to assist and restore them in any way, as well as to remove everything from your life that does not glorify him, and you are asking him to reconstruct your life so that it reflects his glory. This is a prayer that God hears and answers, and He hears and answers prayers like this all the time.

PRAYER DESTINATIONS

1) In the name of Jesus, be blessed with extraordinary miracles and benefits.

2) May your heavenly aid make contact with you right now in the name of Jesus.

3) In the name of Jesus Christ, may the favor of God be upon your life and the lives of your loved ones right now.

Advice On The Art Of Manifestation

I will share with you a method that will help you get in tune with your goals and create them in a way that is harmonious. I have used this method on my own, and I have also had a couple of my customers try it, and everyone of them has had success with it very quickly, so now I want to share it with you!

I went over this with my desired outcomes and I was in detachment and it had precisely the intended impact and as I mentioned I just re-tested it (I had forgotten about it as of not too long ago), and it worked for all of the people who had tried it before. You might also want to note that this is not anything that I came up with on my own; nevertheless, I am unable to give credit to the original author because I have forgotten where I read it in the distant past.

This demonstrates how straightforward and easy manifestation can be, as well as the fact that it does not necessarily have to be a drawn-out process. There is no such thing as "inner healing," "shadow work," or any of the other fancy terminology that people on the internet like to think of as their justifications for not comprehending how to get into alignment. The most important "work" that needs to be done is to gain an understanding of how the universe works and to become conscious, also known as stirring to the way that you make your reality with your thoughts and convictions. This is the primary "work" that needs to be done. Now we're going to get into the good part.

1. Get up and go get a journal for yourself. I strongly suggest that you jot this down in a journal rather than typing it out. It does not have to be anything

elaborate; all that is required is that it address you. If you feel the need to, you can make this journal "your own" by writing your name in it.

2. Make sure you have a good understanding of the following activities and goals that you want to accomplish for yourself.

You have to be persuaded by this, and if you will require a wedding band and a key to his house by tomorrow morning at nine o'clock, then you will most likely have to believe it. I strongly suggest that you begin "little" and gradually work your way up.

6

3. Conceive of what you would like to see unfold over the next three consecutive days, with three different scenarios for

each day. Create this equal affirmation in your current situation over the course of around fourteen days. You may say something like, "I am a money magnet. or I am so happy and grateful now that I live in my dream house with my ultimate lover." as an example. You would repeat that affirmation a number of times in a row, typically three times per day for a period of approximately fourteen days.

While you are writing this, you may experience the feeling of contrast that would be associated with this reality. You should strive to remember your desires in a loving and positive way so that you might evoke feelings of fulfillment inside yourself.

In the unlikely event that it does not work, this WILL be successful. It suggests that you are emitting some form of low frequency when you are confirming, and that this will prevent your manifestation from taking place. After you've calmed down, sat yourself down, taken a few deep breaths, and gotten yourself in a good mood, you may begin writing. This has proved to be effective for me time and time again! Composing and feeling at the same time allows you to efficiently make movements that are both physically and emotionally powerful.

To your success!

Keep A Good Mood And Attitude At All Times

The principle of attraction is not an independent component of the universal law system. It is frequently linked with other universal laws, such as the law of action and the law of karma. Maintaining a good attitude is necessary if you wish to bring wonderful experiences and opportunities into your life.

Proceed with caution.

The principle of attraction is not for those who want everything handed to them without having to put in any effort. In order to bring the things you want into your life, you must also make a conscious effort to bring your goals and desires into fruition. If you put the law of attraction to work for you, the universe will present you with possibilities that will assist you in making your dreams come true. You have no choice but to seize the possibilities presented to you.

Keep in mind that if you are not willing to put in the effort to get what you desire, you will not be successful.

Put an end to your grousing.

Stop being a negative nabob and start making things happen if you want the law of attraction to operate in your favor. It's time to get off your duff. It is important to keep in mind that you must concentrate on the things that you do want rather than on the things that you do not want in order to bring the things you desire into your physical reality.

In instead of concentrating on....

Keep in mind...

The abundance of debt financial resources.

Ailments Physical well-being and overall health

The Problem and Its Solution

Challenges and Unfortunate Events

Many felicitations

The Compliments and the Criticisms

Kindness comes from unexpected places.

Keep in mind that you will receive exactly what you offer. Therefore, if you want to attract all the good things in life, you will also need to engage in acts of kindness that are completely unprompted. You will feel better about yourself as a result of the acts of kindness you perform.

You should assist a new coworker.

Give a call to your parents and inquire about how they are doing.

Purchase some flowers for your sister.

Share with your sweetheart how much affection and appreciation you have for them.

Reassure your children that they are performing their duties admirably.

Prepare a supper for a man who is living on the streets.

You can help other individuals realize their goals by assisting them.

Please assist an elderly lady in crossing the street.

Participate voluntarily in a philanthropic endeavor.

Practice modesty.

Do something kind for another person without expecting anything in return.

Take care not to say anything inappropriate. Share encouraging comments with other individuals to help improve their spirits.

A high frequency of vibration can be attained by maintaining a positive mental attitude. This will make it simpler for the universe to grant your wishes and bring the things you want into your life.

Consider the means through which

It is not enough to simply concentrate on and think about the item you wish to materialize; you will also need to continuously asking yourself how you intend to bring it into existence. You will need to give some thought to the specific actions that you will need to take in order to achieve what it is that you are trying to manifest; otherwise, you will always simply be thinking about it but will never actually take any steps toward achieving it.

Conclusion

I just wanted to take this opportunity to thank you once more for downloading this book. I sincerely want that you have discovered it to be useful and that you have been able to bring more of what it is that you want out of life into manifestation as a result of using it.

The next step for you is to put what you've learned from this book into action so that you can achieve all of your objectives and live the life that you deserve and the life that you want to live. I would ask that you not be bashful about forwarding this information to any members of your immediate family or circle of contacts who you think could find it helpful.

Keep in mind that regardless of where you are in your life right now, it is never too late to start living the life that you deserve to live and to pursue the dreams that you have always wanted to pursue.

Last but not least, if you have read this book and found it to be pleasant, I would be extremely grateful if you would take the time to leave a review on Amazon.com. Thanks so much! It would mean the world to us if you could make it possible!

Confidence In Oneself Is The Source Of The Power To Attract Others.

Most of the time, mental attraction is significantly stronger than its physical counterpart. Even if we close our eyes, we will not be able to protect ourselves from the impact that it has. However, we must first cultivate sufficient levels of self-confidence before we can create this effect. Because there is nothing that draws people in more than the sense that they deserve something.

When discussing this facet, we shouldn't limit our thoughts to seduction, those alluring arts in which cunning tactics can be honed to perfection in order to win over a potential emotional partner.

To gain a job, to bring in new customers, to win over those who are close to us, to leave an impression on a group of people, etc., people need to be able to draw others successfully.

Naturally, we're going to be discussing one's social standing. On the other hand, an essential component that serves as the bedrock of the interesting dimension of attraction power is sometimes disregarded. If we want to leave a good, fascinating, or attractive impression on the people in front of us, we must remember that we must always be true to who we are.

As a result of its inability to stand up to scrutiny, falsehood is characterized by grimaces, false sides, and very little spontaneous Manichaeism. It's not just a cliche to say "always be yourself"; it's good advice.

This term is accurate since there are many more roots that nourish and shape authenticity, including self-assurance, proper personal growth, the belief that we deserve what we want, and the gradual acquisition of a touch of magical ease. A little bit more with experience.

The two peculiar principles governing the strength of attraction

Research in behavioral science is Erin Whitchurch's specialty at the University of Virginia in Charlottesville, where she also teaches. According to her studies in the subject of human attraction, there are two different sorts of laws that will be very intriguing to us and that will explain, in some way or another, many of the sensations that we have all experienced.

The concept of reciprocity

One of the most potent drivers of attraction is the idea of mutual benefit, or the principle of reciprocity. People who think about us and do things for us on the spur of the moment are magnetic to us. This is because we like to be thought about.

They are people who have a great level of emotional openness, who inspire trust, and who, in turn, exhibit genuine reciprocity by accepting to receive but putting an emphasis on contributing.

Lack of assurance

On the other hand, there is some discussion of the uncertainty principle. This law has its roots in physics, but it has relevance in the field of behavioral research as well because it defines something that is at the same time exciting and evident. We are discussing the nearly magnetic pull that a great number of people have on us without our even being aware of it.

They are adept in self-assurance, mystery, and the art of convincing others. They are able to capture our attention since we have no notion what to anticipate from them, which provides our brain with a significant cognitive challenge.

There are three distinct varieties of emotional connections in the realm of the science of attraction.

The realm of feelings is intrinsically related to the power of attraction in some way. The source of this infectious energy, which can be described as engulfing and even hypnotic, can be broken down into three distinct categories of relationships. Several examples of them are as follows:

When I think of confidence and comfort, the terms confidence and comfort are the first ones that spring to my mind. If a person is able to make us feel good, then they have the ability to positively captivate us when they understand how to put into practice an acceptable emotional openness that is built on trust and proximity.

This facet of our life must be accounted for by the presence of emotional intelligence, which is a word that describes a person's capacity to understand and manage their feelings. Empathy, assertiveness, self-esteem, and effective communication skills are "magical" aspects that allow us to connect with others around us, and they feed the power of attraction. Empathy is the ability to feel and understand the emotions and experiences of another person.

The status of having a one-of-a-kind identity is referred to as singularity when discussed using this phrase. It is worked into the framework of the uncertainty principle that governs this dimension. One may consider it to be our official "brand seal." Each of us have "something" inside of us that sets us apart from others and, as a result, makes us unpredictable to others around us.

Locating the specific facet of "power" that best fits our needs can be our biggest source of competitive advantage.

Build up your self-assurance so you can "turn on" your potential to attract others.

Imagine for a moment a land that is completely devoid of vegetation, including trees and flowers. There is no life, nothing beautiful, and only silence can be found here. To cultivate a healthy sense of self-esteem in this parched environment, we must plant a great number of seeds. Because you exude a sense of moderation, security, and charm, these plants will eventually mature and thrive, making you a far more alluring individual over the course of time...

However, what truly makes you strong are the underground roots that provide you stability and tell you daily that you deserve what you desire and that you can achieve it if you set your mind to it. These roots offer you the foundation upon which your strength is built. There you will find the intangible trait of self-confidence, which no one else can see but which you cultivate over time and which you will find there.

In order to accomplish this, take a moment to think about the following dimensions:

Acquire the skill of relying on oneself and being your own source of self-esteem. Nobody needs to tell you how much you are worth or what you deserve. You already know both of those things.

Always be willing to forgive yourself for your mistakes, and remember to give yourself credit for your successes.

Dare to challenge yourself every day by venturing outside of your comfort zone and turning your worries into an obstacle course.

To be able to look at other people with the same amount of admiration, interest, and affection as you direct toward yourself...

Never put on a show that you are someone that you are not since the power of attraction does not work well with dishonesty.

Try, on a daily basis, to identify what distinguishes you from other people, what it is that makes you special and one of a kind, and what sets you apart from the crowd. You'll find the one-of-a-kind feature that gives shape to the concept of uncertainty there, which is so vital in the force of attraction. This is where you'll find it.

Having A Goal In Life While You're Here

Finding out what your life's mission is going to be will be one of your primary objectives. You will work toward the long-term goals by first achieving the shorter-term ones. However, what are some of your individual goals and aspirations? What is it that is preventing you from getting in touch with them?

Your objective will become crystal clear once you realize the answer lies within your own head, rather than in sources found outside of it. Learn more about your true identity. Figure out the reasons behind the decisions you keep making.

The following set of questions is designed to assist you in doing a self-examination and determining your direction in life.

What kinds of events, activities, and hobbies do you like to participate in?

Can you tell me about some of the skills, talents, and abilities you possess?

What are some of the things that you do that cause you to feel proud of yourself?

Do you have any friends or people in your life that you look up to and admire who encourage you to become a better version of yourself? (this is not the same as other people telling you what they think you need to do to improve as a person in accordance with their own opinions. Your own perspectives are solicited in response to this inquiry.)

What is it that you enjoy doing that allows you to completely zone out and forget about anything else?

What do you envision yourself doing when you are an older person, or even when you are an elderly person? Do you want to be able to look back on your achievements, or on the aspirations you never got to fulfill?

Which obstacles have you already surmounted, and which ones are you now attempting to conquer?

What aspects of life are most important to you, and why?

Do you have a strong faith in a particular cause? How exactly do you plan to deepen your involvement with that cause?

How can you help other people by making use of the deeply held ideals and achievements that you have?

You have most likely already come to the conclusion that your life does, in fact, serve a purpose; otherwise, you would not be interested in reading material about living an intentional life. You have already made the decision that in order to obtain success and happiness, you will need to make the required changes. If you did not believe that you had a purpose, it will be twice as difficult for you to discover the kind of personal affirmation that you require in order to lead an effective life. What exactly is the point of that?

You will need to wipe your mental slate clean of everything you have previously believed and begin the process all over again if you want to find out what your purpose is in life. The decisions you've made up to this point in your life will have some bearing on the choices you make in the future; however, you should try to view those experiences from the past as lessons that will help you make better choices in the future. You should never go back to a location that you have already left, and this is especially true if you left the location in a distressing manner. Taking steps in the wrong direction will not help you advance in any way. Let the past go, and focus on moving forward.

It is quite clear that the choices you made in the past were not the wisest ones. You are interested in finding the very best. It's possible that your desires from 10 years ago have evolved, but it's also possible that they haven't. You will be able to evaluate the significance of a goal based on the amount of time you have spent working toward it. If you have a lifelong goal, such as producing a book or climbing a tall mountain, and that goal hasn't altered over the course of your life, then you haven't been taking the appropriate steps to see it come to fruition, else it would have already taken place. As soon as you take that first step toward living a more intentional life, you'll start working toward turning your goals become a reality. You are going to devise strategies in order to achieve that objective. You will eventually figure out what your life's mission is.

You will be responsible for your own personal workout here. This objective for the near future is to take some time to reflect about your life, your aspirations, and the goals you have set for yourself. You could have believed that you knew what your purpose was, but now you can't figure out why you're not satisfied with your life. Evidently, that goal should not have been the focus. Not only will you be able to see clearly what you need in life to be able to say that you are satisfied, at peace, and a contributing member of society, but you will also be able to see clearly what the best way for you to get there is.

One more time, this does not imply that there won't be any challenges or roadblocks along the way. You should expect to encounter detrimental influences, situations, persons, and circumstances along the way. If, on the other hand, you are fully aware of what actions you must do, none of these obstacles will be able to prevent you from continuing on and making progress. They will merely initiate the process of delaying it. How lengthy of a wait there will be is entirely up to your discretion.

It is possible that, for a period of time, you will be required to demonstrate an attitude that some people may characterize as selfish. When someone or something is impeding your progress, unfortunately, it may become necessary to resort to such measures. You have to have a complete understanding of what it is that makes you. To get at this insight, you need to fortify your sense of self, focus on improving any shortcomings you are aware of, and ramp up whatever positive behaviors you already engage in. You are going to be working on yourself, so you can't rely on other people to bring out your mistakes to you. It is essential that you come to the understanding of them within yourself. Your thoughts and actions will be transformed beyond recognition once you reach this level of self-awareness. You will have an understanding of the things that you are unable to achieve and the reasons behind those limitations. You are not going to waste any time deceiving yourself into thinking that something that is not conceivable for you can somehow be made to become a possibility.

Consider how you normally act and break it down. What kind of a reaction do you have when someone criticizes you? What course of action do you take when you have had your trust violated, and you are on the receiving end of contempt and disloyalty? Are you the same person when you're talking to people as when you're by yourself? How do you treat other people in contrast to how it is that you would like to be treated? Which objectives are you working on accomplishing? Finding the answers to these questions can assist you in gaining a better understanding of your individual mission in this life.

Manifesting Joy

One Sunday morning, the significance of gratitude was brought into sharper focus.
Due to the fact that I come from a scientific background, it was difficult for me to believe in the life coach program's process without first conducting experiments, asking questions, and doing research. Over the course of several decades, my brain was conditioned to solve problems by trying new things and relying only on my beliefs.
I made the decision to try out some of the tools and strategies that were presented in the class; in this particular instance, it was keeping a daily thankfulness diary. Because it was impractical for me to bring the leather-bound diary with me everywhere, I decided to keep a digital gratitude

journal instead, which consists of sending a Whatsapp message to myself at regular intervals.

I am more aware of the simple pleasures that life has to offer, such as having hot water in the restroom and eating three freshly prepared meals each day. My parents have made sure that I have everything I need, from a smartphone with strong connectivity to an excellent education. From having a healthy body to being able to get up, breathe, and take in this stunning world, from taking in the smallest things like seeing the sun rise over a snowy landscape in the middle of winter to gazing at the stars in the clear night sky every day, there are countless reasons to be grateful for your life.

I started off by expressing gratitude for each and every blessing in my life. I had completely forgotten that what others covet most is exactly what I already possess. And ever since I made an effort to cultivate an attitude of thankfulness, the universe has showered me with additional reasons to be thankful.

On a certain Sunday morning, I made the decision to bring my kid to the game zone. I offered my sister's children to come with me if they were interested in doing so, but because they were already committed to other obligations, they were unable to do so right away.

When my daughter started having a good time in the game arena, I instantly wrote in my electronic gratitude notebook that I am grateful to the universe for making me successful enough to be able to purchase this joy for my child without having to worry too much about my regular spending habits.

However, after a few minutes had passed, my sister called and informed me that she was going to be leaving both of her children in my care, and that I would be responsible for the upkeep of all three of them. Taking another look at the entries in my gratitude diary, I want to express my appreciation to the universe for making it possible for me to bring joy to not one but two additional children.

The caveat was that in order to receive free tickets that can be redeemed in their store for anything you want to buy, we had to play the game well and get high scores. If we did this, we would be rewarded with free tickets.

The children participated in approximately ten different games and won tickets that could be redeemed for gifts for two younger girls. The gifts consisted of a miniature Barbie coloring box set. The older boy, on the other hand, became a little dejected when he realized that there were no gratis tickets available to be redeemed.

I encouraged him to participate in one more game so that he might win tickets for himself, and although he was a champion and won many tickets, he was still behind by ten tickets. I did not want to give him the impression that we had nothing in common. I came to the conclusion that the best way to show my appreciation was to play one game for him, collect as many free tickets as I could, and purchase the item he had his eye on, which turned out to be a leather cricket ball.

I then began to play the game, and it was at this precise moment that the cosmos began to work in my favor. I swiped the playing card for the very final time, and then I began the game.

Not only did I get the top score (which I was meant to get because it was a kids zone), but the redeem ticket vending machine went into hyperactive mode and started pumping out complimentary tickets like they were going out of style. This was a great fact. We did end up waiting for the gadget to stop for a full three minutes, at which point we gleefully collected our freebie tickets following the intervention of the shop employee. I'm still not sure whether the vending machine genuinely broke or whether I just achieved the best score and there were a few extra tickets left over as our share of the spoils. I came to the conclusion that I should capitalize on the uncertainty and put thankfulness in the driver's seat instead.

We were taken aback when we discovered that we needed only ten more tickets in order to purchase the leather cricket ball; however, we were given 1500 tickets instead.

The happiness that came from receiving more than was requested was incomparable. We got the little ladies two different stationery sets, a writing board, a pencil case, and a sharpener in addition to the leather cricket ball. Due to his advanced age, the child had little choice but to make do with his trusted ball and pencil.

We left the location with smiles on our faces and happiness in our hearts and hands. The amount of money we lost playing the games has been more than recouped by the presents we were given. Now that I've applied the teachings from the course and am writing my letter of thanks, I understand that this was the ideal example of practicing gratitude and receiving more than what one had asked for.

In the evening, when I was still lost in my cheerful thoughts, I related the experience to my mother. And as a result of having been raised in a typical Indian household of the middle class, she simply stated that the gifts were not deserving of money, which has resulted in all of us becoming really happy.

At the time, I chose to be quiet out of respect for my mother; nonetheless, my heart frequently questioned the decisions I was making. Is it possible to put a price on the excitement, happiness, and pure adrenaline rush that we felt while playing or while watching the ticket vending machine go ga ga?

We are all the sum total of our upbringings; more or less, as we become older, we begin to believe in the lessons that were taught to us by our parents. Then, did our parents make a mistake when they conditioned our minds to be in the "saving mind" mode or the "achieving particular thing" mode, and then they put us in the "celebrating mode"?

Or shall we blame ourselves for refusing to mature and refuse to accept one hundred percent responsibility for our very own fantasy life? Do we, as mature persons, put in enough effort to change the beliefs, conditioning, or nurture that we were brought up with? Do we take a moment to appreciate either the process or the journey? Or are we continuing the race that has been passed down from generation to generation, measuring happiness in terms of the things that money can buy? Do we educate our children or ourselves that happiness is not a state of being but rather a decision that can be made? Are we truly paying attention to the minor joys that we encounter each and every day, or are we too busy feeding our thoughts, beliefs, conditioning/rules/expectations, and always placing pressure on ourselves?

When I found myself lost in the conflict between my mind and my heart, the only thing I could come to the conclusion of was that the self-imposed prison of my pride and prejudice was preventing me from making progress, and that this was the area in which the greatest amount of effort was required.

It's not that I didn't have this knowledge before; of course, similar conflicts had arisen many times when I was growing up. However, the new insight was that despite being conscious of my ideas, I invariably end up falling prey to them, resulting in a victim mindset. This is not to say that I didn't have this knowledge before. I don't even recall how many times life has given me the opportunity to laugh and have a good time, and I don't remember the sorrows that I've had, with the exception of a select few.

All that I can recall is that I was constantly on the lookout for reasons. But now I see that it is not necessary for the reason to be present in its physical form for it to be valid. It may have been a post on social media, a book, a movie, an image, a concept, or even an encounter. I came to the conclusion that the universe should be the source of my utmost joy, and I should give up all control to it.

Oh, I totally forgot to say that we could simply buy the items that we won, but do you know what made them more valuable? It was the process!!

In a different instance, I began putting the ideas of Arigato money and the law of abundance into practice without first waiting for my hopes and dreams to be realized. And when I started donating money with an abundance mindset, the universe began to shower me with abundance in return.

A girl was receiving some of my used clothing donations when all of a sudden she asked for 10 rupees.

I quickly took out 10 rupees and gave them to the girl before my conscious mind could take over and tell me to "give food over money" or any of the other chatterbox talks.

I gave her something, and in exchange I got to see the wonderful smile on her face. She wished me farewell and invited me to visit once more.

It was only ten rupees to me, but for her, it represented an incalculable amount of delight.

If you give, you will receive; in this case, the reward came in the form of an irreplaceable smile.

It is said that if you ask for something, it will be given to you, and she requested the cosmos for 10 rupees, and the universe granted her desire and handed her exactly 10 rupees.

How To Bring More Money Into Your Life Is A Step-By-Step Guide

Who doesn't wish they had a lot of money, though, right? We are all taught, and research has shown, that money cannot buy happiness, and this is true. On the other hand, money may buy comfort, and feeling comfortable can be a factor in one's level of happiness and contentment.

Here are the steps to take if you want to employ the law of manifestation to bring in more money into your life:

Take a stand - You must take a stand and determine that from this day forward, you want your life to be characterized by a greater abundance of money. In order to bring in more money in your life, you need to actually feel the strong impulse and want to do so.

Take a good hard look at your worldview. The concept of money can evoke strong feelings. When the topic of money is brought up in any discussion, individuals experience a variety of feelings. You have to get rid of the negative thoughts that you have about money if you want to make it easier for money to manifest in your life. There are others who are under the impression that in order to get wealthy, one must resort to dishonesty and criminal activity. The majority of individuals have the limiting notion that it is difficult to become wealthy, and as a result, they have never made an attempt to increase the amount of money in their lives. To bring more money into your life, you must first feel at ease around it. You have to have the mindset that wealth represents something positive in your life.

Spend some time reflecting about your financial situation and the things you could buy if you had an endless supply of cash. This will help you determine how you feel about money. Are you experiencing any unease? Do you have any feelings of guilt? Do you have feelings of unworthiness? Are you pleased with how you feel and at ease?

If the idea of having more money makes you feel uneasy, you can rewire your mindset by meditating frequently and repeating positive affirmations. This will make it possible for your subconscious to be more receptive to the concept of having more money.

The following are some of the affirmations that you should say to yourself on a regular basis in order to assist you in the process of manifesting additional money into your life. Creating your own personal affirmations is always an option. Act in a way that is suitable for you.

Having money is a positive thing.

I am able to quickly and easily attract monetary resources.

I am putting away more and more cash as each day passes.

My financial situation continues to improve, and as a direct result, I no longer have any outstanding debt.

The sum of money in my bank account continues to rise on a daily basis without fail.

I have positive feelings about money and believe that I am entitled to have more of it.

There is no upper limit to the amount of money that I am capable of acquiring.

Keep in mind that the power of an affirmation is magnified when it is spoken with conviction. It is in your best interest to reiterate these comments once per day for the next three months. If you do this, it will assist you in reprogramming your mindset and belief system.

Write down how much money you want to have and when you want to have it by. Write down how much money you want to have and when you want to have it. Because this will be a signal that you send out into the universe, having specifics is very crucial. This will help you manifest what you desire more quickly.

In the early 1980s, when Jim Carrey was still a struggling actor who was trying to make ends meet, he scribbled down a check for 10 million dollars and carried the check in his pocket. When he finally got his big break, he cashed the check for 10 million dollars. He dated the check with the year 1995. Indeed, in the latter half of 1994, he received a paycheck of ten million dollars for his performance in the film "The Dumb and the Dumber."

Imagine that you already had that much money in your bank account right now. Take some time out of your day, close your eyes, and imagine that you already have that amount of money. What are you going to get? How do you plan to utilize it? Taking this action will result in positive emotions and vibrations, and it will also assist you in more rapidly materializing the things you seek.

Have faith and believe that you will obtain the sum of money that you have been hoping for. Get rid of any lingering uncertainties and have unyielding and firm conviction that you are deserving of being given that sum of money.

Inspired Action - Once you have a solid faith that what you want will materialize, you will start to become aware of chances that will enable you to acquire the sum of money that you want to materialize in your life. Always keep in mind that you should make the most of possibilities like these. These opportunities can present themselves in the shape of new initiatives, new commercial opportunities, or a promotion. When an opportunity presents itself, seize it with both hands!

How Can One Make The Most Out Of Manifestation Strategies To Maximize Their Benefits?

You need to do a lot of research so that you won't become disheartened in the event that you don't achieve your goals even if you tried your best. You can start working on your own strategy for personal development with the assistance of the following guidelines, which are presented below. You need to gain an understanding of what motivates you in order to achieve your goals. Even while the recommendations of others can be helpful, you shouldn't be surprised if something that functions well for other people does not work well for you. After you have gained an understanding of what motivates you, you will be in a position to devise a system of rewards for yourself that will assist you in remaining focused on your objective. Try as hard as you can to stay away from substances that stimulate the nervous system. The term "stimulants" refers to a group of substances that include coffee, other caffeinated beverages, and even nicotine.

These factors have an effect on the amount of fat you can burn. Even while this may not always be a negative aspect, you still need to be aware of the fact that it has the potential to be. In the event that you find yourself in an unpleasant disposition, you ought to investigate the manner in which you use animates in a significantly more careful way. In the event that the circumstances are not developing in the manner in which you had hoped for them to, you should halt what you are doing and reevaluate your strategy. In the event that you have prepared a setup that is not successful, you should rewrite that gets ready and make the necessary adjustments that will assist in changing the consequence. It is possible that it will call for a significantly increased investment; nonetheless, in spite of all the effort, it will be justified. Maintain a modern approach to both your methods and your strategies. It doesn't matter what you want to do in your life, one thing you should always remember to do is to be creative in your approach. Being creative in your approach may really help in encouraging success more effectively and accepting a higher degree for the things that you are doing.

You need to have suggestions based on recommendations, and this sometimes implies that you need to think viable outside of the box into the creative area. Figure out how to tap into the aspects of yourself that you have ignored in the past. You should really try to obtain a deep look at both your spirit and your soul. Just make sure you have a clear understanding of who you are. In the event that you are unaware of the resources at your disposal, it will be impossible for you to implement any private changes. Take this seriously, and be open to the fact that a variety of different sentiments may surface throughout the process. Checking your day-to-day activities is an important part of the self-backing process.

One useful piece of advice for aiming to bring more attention to yourself is as follows:

Instead of being fixated on a single, individual point of view, make an effort to examine a situation from a variety of perspectives. Reading the cognitive processes of different people groups can provide knowledge to your own in areas that you may not have previously had prior experience in. Are you considering the ways in which you can create as a unique individual? Help out other people by doing things for them! Helping other people makes people happier and makes them feel better about themselves. This is true for both men and women, but it is especially true for those who lend a helping hand to others. Being able to verify anything by assisting a variety of people. It takes the purpose away from you and places it on someone else's shoulders instead. If you do so, you will feel even better about the fact that you have made somebody else feel more significant and have contributed to making their day special.

The final word

Due to the fact that there is virtually no experimental evidence to support any of these claims, researching this topic may be quite challenging and mind-boggling at the same time. When we first get interested in something, it is almost always only speculation, with only a trace amount of evidence drawn from scientific research. However, the way I look at it, if it doesn't hurt you, there is no reason why you shouldn't go up against it on the board. If it doesn't hurt you, then there is no reason why you shouldn't go up against it. It won't hurt you to think decisively, and it definitely won't hurt you to try your hand at higher levels of consciousness either. Both of these things won't hurt you. It won't make a difference even if this alters the vitality frequencies that you anticipate sending out into the world and, as a result, brings you more good fortune and favorable luck. It is in everyone's best interest to think more decisively and to make every effort to come into contact with the highest levels of consciousness. That is probably where the greatest amount of happiness and contentment can be discovered. Why not make accomplishing it your primary goal then?

It is essential, however, to emphasize the fact that all of the rich and enchanted information that we covered in this section is inextricably woven into your consciousness. As a result of this, your convictions, values, contemplations, self-idea, mental guidelines, human needs, meta-projects, and all of the other components of your mind each have a unique vitality mark that is expected to be released into the world once every day. In addition to this, as a result, it is quite important to arrange the process of introducing the basic changes to these aspects of your mind. Simply by proceeding in this manner, you will be able to properly move the vitality frequencies that you are anticipating out into the universe. Therefore, in the event that you are under the impression that any of this is true, you are not. Ignore all that has been stated here and concentrate solely on improving specific aspects of your mind. Focus your attention on overcoming the limiting beliefs and unproductive thoughts that you now have. Focus your attention on modifying your characteristics, mental standards, human requirements, and meta-programs. In addition, you should work on improving your self-idea, mental self-portrait, and self-regard, as well as building up your joyful adapting skills.

You will change as you progress through each of these areas, and so will your life, on account of the fact that the vitality you are projecting into the world at this point is different from what it was before. In addition, as the state of your vitality shifts, you will consequently attract other comparable energies that are consistent with the state of your vitality. It's possible that just doing that will be the quickest and most effective way to move up the awareness level.

You are now in possession of the resources and knowledge necessary to do everything that you require; nevertheless, it is solely up to you to put these into action and actually incorporate them into your daily life. That is the primary route that will lead to success... The reading by itself won't be of any use to you in any way... It's possible that every once in a while, we'll all feel gloomy... You won't, however, remain defeated if you adhere to the advice given above; this is true regardless of how challenging life may be for you. You are going to be successful in overcoming every challenge, and you WILL arrive at your destination!

Message No. 8: It Is Time to Create Your Own Manifesting Rules! The Law of You! (Simply Because It Is Possible!)

How can one most effectively bring the life they love into existence? What exactly is the biggest hidden truth? How do you locate the most helpful instructor or guide for your path towards LOA? What are some good books and other resources to look into? Attending such events or working with a manifestation coach can be a good idea for you.

When there are so many different roads you could take, it's easy to get confused!

The majority of people nowadays are looking for the most effective and quickest route to accomplishing their objectives. We certainly do comprehend the fact that you wish to bring the objects of your desires into existence as soon as humanly possible. Why in the world wouldn't you? The upbeat news is that the answer is yes, you absolutely can. Your requests can be answered in the blink of an eye by the universe. That shouldn't be a problem at all. However, keep in mind the following point. Things move more slowly because the all-knowing Universe is aware that you have specific lessons to learn before you may expand to your full potential. Never give up on being the embodiment of your truth. Have confidence in the procedure!

There is no definitive right or wrong answer when it comes to selecting a classroom setting, a textbook, or a subject to study. Listen to your intuition, and make a conscious decision to gain knowledge from people whose energy align with your own. It can be summed up like that.

Also, keep in mind the spiritual reality that you are responsible for the creation of the Law of You. Yes, it is possible to study several spiritual principles, such as the Law of Attraction, the Law of Assumption, the Law of Gratitude, and other similar laws, and to learn about these laws from a variety of teachers. We are inspired by your enthusiasm for self-improvement and learning, and we strongly recommend that you continue down the path of personal development.

However, keep in mind that the most important legislation is the law that governs you. Because your own energy is what will bring the life you want into manifestation! You can get some direction and some actions to follow as well as some frameworks to follow from authors, coaches, and teachers. However, the path that you choose to pursue throughout your adventure is entirely up to you at all times.

What you accept as true is ultimately determined by your beliefs. It begins to be the truth for you in the reality that you experience.

When Elena first started out on her adventure, she was thrown for a loop because the LOA community is full of apparent inconsistencies. She endeavored to work out the proper procedure and was intent on locating the best instructor. However, she quickly saw that there was no cause for concern.

They learned the spiritual principles, put those rules into practice, and discussed what had been successful for them. Now, Elena continues to approach things in the same manner. She publishes articles in which she discusses and imparts information on various ways and strategies that she has found to be successful. She is of the opinion that it is a wonderful method for her readers to begin. However, she is always encouraging them to choose their own paths, act as their own instructors and mentors, and compose their own stories for their lives.

You have the last word on this matter. You have the option to take what you learn and either embrace it or reject it. You need to awaken the mentor that resides within you. That voice deep within you that encourages you to do well and wishes nothing but the best for you. That will watch out for you at all times and care for you just like a parent would. You are able to calm your inner state and continue going forward even if things do not proceed in the direction that you had hoped for, without experiencing feelings of disappointment or resentment.

We want you to look at LOA in a fresh light and approach it in the following ways: through living it, testing it, and embodying it. Additionally, place your emphasis on the things that are successful for you. It is important to show gratitude to those who have taught you something as well as to learn from others. However, you may contribute by deciding to be the person you are.

Accept and Embrace the Law That Is You. Have the confidence to write your own set of guidelines. Developing your own set of guidelines is not just acceptable but encouraged!

For instance, Elena made the decision not too long ago (we touched on this in the section regarding negative ideas) that only her good thoughts will appear. This is something that she shares, as well as something that she believes in. It IS her truth, after all! It not only made her feel liberated from negative ideas, but it actually made her feel free! She only made the decision that negative thoughts would have no influence on her and that she would only see the results of her good thinking. She instituted it as her own rule. She is just beginning to share it with others in the hopes of being an inspiration to them.

Where do you stand? Are you able to make up your own guidelines? You have the ability to choose the strategies and ways of manifestation you want or do not prefer. You are free to pick the strategies that are effective for you, study them, put them to the test, and then advance them to the next level. Intellectual familiarity with each individual is not required. You only need to take things slowly and carefully, and keep putting different rules and regulations to the test. Oh, and have we not yet mentioned that there is no way for you to fail? There is no such thing as failure; there is only feedback. There is no such thing as that. Either you are successful or you learn. That brings us to the conclusion!

Make yourself into a law unto yourself. Create your own procedures for manifestation right this moment. As long as you are not causing harm to other people and are acting in accordance with your genuine inclinations, you are set to go.

So, what do you think it would be like to act as your own guide and instructor? What about developing your very own strategy for manifestation?

Last but not least, allow us to remove one more obstacle in the way of your manifestations: "What will other people think of me?"

Put it out there right this minute and right here. The realities of other people are created by the imaginations of those other people. But at this very moment, assuming that we haven't got it all wrong, we are discussing your reality, right?

And your thoughts, not the thoughts of others, are what bring your reality into being, is that correct?

Therefore, just be yourself. Accept and Embrace the Law That Is You. Allow yourself the luxury of simply existing as you are. You are the one who writes the story for your life, but we will always be here to help guide you.

www.ingramcontent.com/pod-product-compliance
Lightning Source LLC
Chambersburg PA
CBHW050236120526
44590CB00016B/2107